KISSED BY A FAT WAITRESS

New Poems

Dan Fante

1/10/10

Dnt Born
This

Best
Dan

2008
Sun Dog Press
Northville, Michigan

Kissed By a Fat Waitress

Copyright © 2008 by Dan Fante

Cover design by Grey Christian

Book design by Judy Berlinski

Illustrations by Allen Berlinski

The publisher wishes to thank *Beat Scene, Ten Point Press, Bottle of Smoke, X-Ray Book Co.,* and *Bottle Rockets* where some of these poems first appeared. Some of the drawings first appeared in Irving Stettner's *Stroker* magazine.

Published by Sun Dog Press
22058 Cumberland Dr.
Northville, MI 48167

arberlin@twmi.rr.com

Library of Congress Control Number: 2008920275

ISBN 978-0-941543-47-7

Manufactured in the United States of America   First Edition

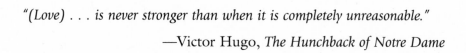

"(Love) . . . is never stronger than when it is completely unreasonable."

—Victor Hugo, *The Hunchback of Notre Dame*

CONTENT

Mom at eighty-nine

Today
at the home
I read her some of my new stuff
while she squinted at me—straining to hear

My savvy mouth
sputtering out
chainsaw syllables
beneath those perfect and unspoiled steel-grey eyes

This ancient ex-editor
who's read more and knows more about writing and poetry
than I'll ever hope to know

Five minutes in to it looking up—I said—"Well, whaddya think?"

She seemed distracted
ten thousand brow wrinkles came—flattened out—then returned

"Do you still have that phone sales job," she said—

"No Ma, I don't have a day gig anymore—writing is all I do now"

"Well get one, for chrissake," she said—"and help me up—
I need to use the bathroom"

the market

I ran into old Don
today
still checking at the Ralphs on Sepulveda Boulevard
after 25 big ones—

Looks like—just for a change—the boss is screwing them again on
their pension plan
and the picketing they did and the strike that time
and that two hour speech from the honcho from the A F-of-L
all didn't do nobody no goddamn good whatsoever

because the working stiff is still the lowest lizard on the food chain

But old Don's doesn't care—says he's retiring at the end of the year
no matter what

Says he's gonna spend full time at that place he built in Mexico
and slam his insulin twice a day
and fish until his fingers fall off

And I'm cranking the starter in my Chevy out in the parking lot
when it hits me

I've been doing the only thing I ever wanted to do
—daily—
for almost twenty years
no union—no paid vacations—no OT
and no shit

I still can't get enough

anniversary

Today it's ten years—to the day—since my big brother Nick
cashed in
in the ER
and caught his cab

Nick Fante—the genius artist
55 years old
Nick who designed the feet of the Lunar Landing Craft and
at nine was a chess champion and then had scholarships to every art
school in L.A. before he even left grammar school

Nick—tubes and gizmos running in and out of every hole after forty
years of booze and four pints of his ruptured blood
puddling up
on a white Spanish tile ER floor

Vodka was Nick's life-long lover and the key lubricant that propelled
his path to the boneyard
and not a one of the handful of thirty thousand dollar 28-day drip-dry
whoop-de-do fuckin' in-patient cures he took
ever worked
to
help him soothe his scalding brain
for having had sex with his 12-year-old daughter
one sleepy L.A. summer night
in a blackout

Nick Fante never got passed it or over it
or would talk about it
and he finally collected all that pain and took it down
with him
into the cold wet dirt—leaving me—right here

today

still

missing
him
like hell

asking

For years I thought that
talking to the Gods
was an exercise
done privately
under
unforgiving

distant stars

ridiculous unrequited prayer
done by staring
at old cold books
with mean small print

But then I discovered
that just
ain't
it at all

God can be found in the "thank you" voice of the guy at the counter
at the 7-11
or
the quietness of a stranger's parking lot smile
or
the rattle of weeds across a dry summer Mojave
or
watching my untethered fingers jump jump jumping
across the keys
deep in the middle of typing three hours worth of truth

God—for me—turned out to be
a conscious choice
a self-evoked experience

just
like
love

dear editor:

You complete idiot moron asshole dufus—
do you actually believe that what writers do—what I do—is some sort
of disposable—quick-trick slight-of-hand mechanical keyboard
flim-flam
like the shuffling of a deck of cards or lip-syncing my novel into a
computer program or punching a goddamn GPS address into the
dashboard of your powder blue ninety-thousand-dollar 4-door BMW

Next time—
dear subhuman thoughtless editor—
when we meet
when I submit something I've written to you
maybe
I'll simply stand on your desk and press a gun barrel between your
wide-set eyes
so we can have a real conversation called
what I do as an artist is cut away pieces of myself and smear those
dripping chunks of flesh
across a page so that anyone willing enough—tuned-in enough—
to connect their mind with mine
can see inside
my
heart

Believe it or not dear editor—
I do not give a rat's dick whether my rejected new book of stories
fits into your projections for next year's publication list
or
not

You may trust this:
I will continue to do as I have always done—
to open myself up as much as I can—to tear away at my own
self-importance and delusion
a layer at a time
and to seek and speak my deepest
and closest truth

until

15

the day my wife
and kid
pack my body in dry ice
sew my lips and eyes closed
and file my stinking remains
in the breakwater off Santa Monica Pier

And one last thing Dear Editor:
thanks
again
for
taking
your
time
to
consider
my
work

Melrose Avenue at four a.m.

Blood everywhere
on the car's seat
on the floorboard

and me
still half wasted
freaked and desperate and helpless
saying stuff like—it's okay—you're gonna be okay—we'll be there in a
minute—
just hang on for godsake

and more blood

Your shirt and pants sopped by it
your face white . . . going porcelain

with an entire liver puked up—on the floor of my car

Hang on, goddamnit! Can you just hang on?

"I'm hanging on, fucker . . . drive faster"

And all the love and all the lies of our friendship
the years of our days and nights together
have
devolved
to this
last careless reckless ride in Hollywood

Okay . . . okay . . . we're here . . . can you hear me?

kissing your head as they wheeled you in
but
only later remembering
I
never
really
stopped to say goodbye

8-30-07

I've got no idea
why
love's been so random for me
chaotic even

a busted slot machine

a wet kiss from a fat waitress

why what my eyes have bitten into
and hungrily devoured
inevitably—invariably—tasted sour

why my gut instincts have never been other than
100% flawlessly flawed
and infallibly inaccurate

why I've allowed my ass to be harpooned and deep fried again and
again at pissy property settlement meetings
and carnivorous divorce proceedings
then permitted
less than zero
to be a perfect math calculation

entirely fucking okay

until
U
baby—until you—
and the surprisingly
wondrous
miraculous
sweet
dripping
taste
of
cherry
pie

2-15-07

My birthday's coming up
in a few days

The big six-three

and the first forty-five of those years were spent tussling within myself
struggling—rooting through rotted bones in an attempt to reveal a
purpose
that—try as I might—
never
appeared

Drunk—cleaning my .357—yearafteryear I'd ask myself . . . ."why do
this?"
—it's pointless . . . painful

and the answer'd come back—"you're right—fuck it!"

And that's how I was
—nothing at all left to lose

except my life

Until I began
to
write
and the world turned
from shit brown to pink cotton candy

and my heart broke and healed and broke again—as I continued to
unclog my smothered heart
and
to finally become a real—no-shit—no-kidding
living human being

springtime for Fante

Last night
at dinner with a guy from the *L.A. Times*
I found out that I'm the subject of a major story
next month

Thaz right
ME
eight pages of text and photos inside their Sunday Weekend
Magazine

Me
who has sold a grand total of six thousand books
in America over the last fifteen years

Me
with all my shit basically out-of-print

Me
who long ago dreamed of fame and sweet
breast-augmented actresses
tenderly enjoying my winkie
until
I gave up
and went the-fuck-back to phone sales

Me
a famous writer?

Sure sure sure

I mean, why not
I'm not dead yet—
or in jail
so
why
not
ME
shit happens, right?

customer service

This morning I dialed the 800 number and after ten minutes on hold
I get some ditz bitch named La Donna on the line
all the way in the Philippines
to fix
the current bogus charges on my Visa card

the overbilling—from the dinner I bought the old lady for our
anniversary at The Asylum Restaurant in
Jerome, Arizona six weeks ago

But see—La Donna—after additional hold time—in her heavy Tagalog
accent gets back to me and says she can't help me because she sees I've
moved but neglected to update my *primary account information* with
Chase-fuckin-Card Services
so
therefore
I'm S O L
and
ain't nothin'—not a goddamn thing that La Donna's in Manila is
gonna do for me
until I call the 877 number she's giving me now and speak to
Milton
who after more minutes on hold tells me he'll be glad as all hell and
delighted to help me provided of course I'm aware that my open
account of 14 years ago still has a different address than my current
fucking whereabouts
which I of course know already
and is the reason I called in the first place and is the reason I'm
calling
so—Milton says—until that account and my address are correctly
updated ain't a goddamn thing he can do for me either—
the current charges on your account are status quo sir because
—see—you have not answered the secret question which is:
what was your address 14 years ago!!!

So I slam the receiver down and try to remember that I'm over twenty
years without a drink in my hand
and that there are *"no big deals"* and that *"tomorrow's another day"*—

and *"live and let live"*—
and *first things first*—
and *you can't think yourself into right acting—you have to act yourself into right thinking*

I mean
what really is the goddamn point in throwing an eighty-nine ninety five battery phone against a wall and watching the thing blast apart into a thousand tiny pieces

I mean how childish can you get?

WELL—THE POINT IS—
IT FUCKIN' HELPS
THAT'S
THE
FUCKING
POINT !!!!!!!!!!!!!!

my seventh seal

One time—years ago—I
met Bergman
the
Swedish filmmaker guy

I was limo-ing in Manhattan
at it
seventy to eighty hours a week
and staying stinking drunk when I wasn't in my vested polyester suit
and chauffeur's cap

Ingmar was a humble cat
in his plaid shirt and khaki pants
speaking in measured—perfect—schoolroom English
as we drove the city streets together

seeing New York—he said—through my eyes—
Up and down the island for hours
South Ferry and back
The Bronx—the docks—East Harlem

When we were done I said
"So what do you think of New York"

The shy man thought about it for a few seconds then smiled—
"I live on a tiny piece of land in the Baltic," he said—"I see five
houses, the sea, and only my dogs for eleven months a year
and cities, for me, are an excess—an overdose of humanity—like
falling into a freezing river"

Do you drink, I asked

Sometimes—he said—I drink sometimes

Drinking warms up the water—I said
drinking
really helps

5-24-04

So this is it

holy Christ!

Finally
at my age

ONE YEAR!
the
unpredictable
impossibility of a happy marriage

Daily
I get up
drink my coffee and sit at my keyboard
reliving my twenty years of near death bottled-in-bond insanity
ranting my rants
while you
from work
send me your intermittent e-mails
about loving me
and great sex
and the joy at having my kid about to pop out of your belly

And I think
Jesus
I'm sixty years old
let me die now
before I fuck this up too

I never had anything this good

And all the time knowing that what I really want is
more
more
more

never satisfied

I
always
wanted more

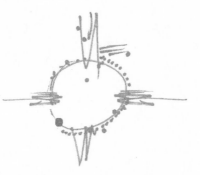

Filled
one glass
then
immediately
wanted
another

until you

you

one look
at
you

and I drowned my heart in a river of stars

the kid

My son Giovanni's in the other room
as I sit here typing—wrenching my brain

Hearing him in there
eighteen months old
pushing his red bus across the carpet
into
the wall
again and again—bam bam, bam bam
making up chatter-box words
in an unknown one-way conversation
as he goes

One-hundred percent present
in
the
moment

complete crunching bliss

And all
I'll ever want
is
to
be just like
that kid

in the now—always—
nothing added

Totally
with
God

the comedian

Last night
at a theater
in
Hollywood
I
saw my pal Mike's one-man stand-up show

He's sober—years sober in fact
and has won an Emmy as a sit-com genius
and his rage at life and at failed bitter love
and parenthood
was overwhelming to sixty seared spectators
sitting in damn near dead silence
for seventy five fucking minutes
of hugely
unfunny
pain

Later—I made a foolish wrong turn
and there I am
standing in his formica-paneled one-neon bulb dressing room
with no available get-away route

Mike's desperate for some kinda atta boy for his one-trick rant
and for no good reason whatever I tell him the truth—
"I didn't laugh,"
—"it made me sad," I say—"I'm sorry"

So now here's Mike
his fifty-year-old burned-down face deflated
instantaneously dead

rendered speechless

And sixth seconds later I'm heading down the hall
toward the parking lot
telling myself
nice work asshole
when—in your elongated thoughtless ill-considered moronic life—
are you going to learn not to tell people

how you feel
and make a fresh start at not losing friends

Hypocrisy and a blow job
are what gets a man to heaven
in
Los Angeles

the truth is a rotting stinking dead cat
sealed up in the wall behind your bed
a
painful
and
pointlessly useless
fairy
tale

lemme alone

The goddamn phone
keeps ringing

People—workmen and neighbors and god knows who –
bang on my door
wanting Christ knows what

this
and
that

The old lady leaves a note
"remember to take my boots to the leather guy and put the baby's
sheets in the dryer"

And I
—strapped in—
sit here
after almost all these years off the juice
trying to write—to make some meaning of old madness

suddenly realizing
just ONE pop—a little eye-opener
just might take the edge off

Just ONE

Knowing all the time that
just ONE
is exactly the distance for me back to the blackness of the nut ward

Yet some days
just ONE
sounds
sooooooooo
goddamn
good

Hubert Selby, Jr.—4-27-04

Cubby died last night
when I got the news—felt the screws—
I had to sit down because it was as if
someone had punched me in the stomach

Selby was
my miracle
my icon
my model of a writer
my mentor
my how-to

From Selby I'd learned to spill my guts and open my heart on paper
and to become not just another mouth in search of a scream

Year ago and newly off blended whiskey I'd followed Cubby around to
his L.A. readings

stalking the guy—even

waiting outside every bookstore door until he'd busted-out his last
autograph and was lugging his big box of books back to his car

and when I'd finally gotten up the guts to ask him to read the fat
unstapled manuscript in my hand that had by then been rejected by—
deemed unprintable—by not less than thirty of the best-est most
brilliant-est bubble-brained-est bozo publishing minds in the city of
New York

So two months later I'm coming home after fourteen hours at my car
sales job to click on the red blinking button
and hear his gaspy raspy voice on my answering machine
for the first of a thousand replays until the tape wore out
as he whispered . . .

Hey Dan Fante—this is Cubby—
Cubby Selby
Hey—that's one helluva book you wrote
I mean—man, it hit me in the heart and wouldn't let me go—
and while I was reading it I kept saying to your guy Bruno
Oh no, man . . . don't do that

Oh no, man . . . no no—don't tell her that—you can't say that
I mean—Christ—what a book!
So you just keep writing Fante
keep making the magic
that's great stuff
really great stuff
you'll get there—I mean it
I'll see ya around Fante

And it was Selby
in one phone call
who passed the gift of his writer's courage
on to me
to not give up
to just keep going
to send my stuff out again and again

It was Selby—Selby was my God

So no matter what any newspaper says about his death
or where they plant his skinny bones
I'll just blink
or read one of the quotes tacked to my office wall
and the spark in my heart will glow again and I will smile
and my life as a writer will be full
all because of you, Cubby

because
of
you

for Ayrin

I am
a reflection of

your will

you stopped me – spun me like a top –
pulled me in – like a soppy Hollywood movie

it's taken me years to realize
to
understand – finally -
that single thing that
rescued
me from my own madness and aloneness
and stopped
the non-stop screaming of
my
self

in a single kiss

It
was
you babee

it
was
truly

only
you

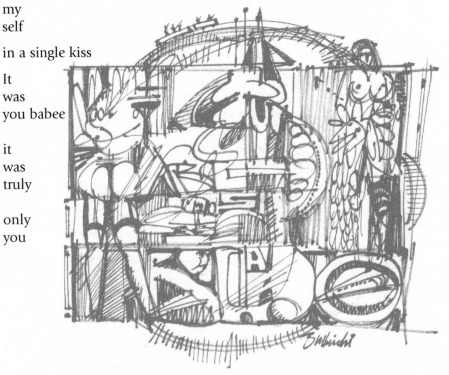

say it loud, Jack

Today
my magazine friend
in England
Kevin
sent me a note wanting me to write a few hundred words
a sort-of commemoration
of 37 years after the death of Jack Kerouac

So I wrote back later telling him "sure, okay"—no problem
then took a long sip of my morning espresso
and—the obvious—
hit me

that there'd be no Bukowski, no Selby, no Carver
not
a one of us

without whacked Jack

without his bad luck and booze and self hate
and Oedipal weirdness
and a heart slashed heal-less by passion and rage and madness and
pain
and
that
need
he
always
had
to
tear things open and burn them down—and start again

So Jesus Christ—thanks Jack
my life as an artist
the thousands of hours of me feeling the angels singing through my
heart and hands
would be

nowhere

down the shitter
without
your
voice
and
your
arrogant
and
amazingly
beautiful
twisted
smile

test results

My blood pressure is
122 over 80

My
fighting weight
is 158

I'm there

I swim 20 laps three times a week
and
at over sixty I'm still

a pretty decent "stick" man

between
the
sheets

But the older you get—there's no way around the truth
that is
the black dots on the screen are getting closer and closer

And on the days I stop
occasionally
to add up my life
I always
wonder
how I got this lucky

how a shitsucking loser like me
—counted out—
and left for dead
could
have
any
excuse for
not laughing his ass off

long live L.A.

Today
I hung up
after a thirty minute conversation
with an L.A. movie producer
about a screenplay

and
felt my heart hammering in my chest

What was that—I said
what in the blithering Jesus fuck was that conniving prick trying to sell
me

And I had no idea whatever
not one clue

I know only this:
there is nothing more soul-less and godless on the planet
than a Hollywood film producer

Give me Mother Teresa on crack with an ice pick in her paw

Ohhhh dear Jesus
hear my prayer
save me from these
soul-less dogshiteatingmotherfuckers

except
of
course

on payday

last night

Little Giovanni was tucked away in his crib
and the TV news was on
and
Ayrin
pulled me close
where I could smell the warm
mustiness
of her—the touch of her
amazing
skin

and—whispered to me
that
she's pretty sure she's pregnant
again

Ohhhhhhhhhhhhhhhhhhhhhhh I said
clicking the remote clicker . . . casually
hiding my head behind a pillow
that's great news, babee

and alla time thinking
here I am
a wet-eyed
sixty-two years old grandpa
with a reconstituted life
loving it
almost
every
second

I'm alive . . . and not yet completely
scared
to
death

two survivors

Twenty-five years ago
sputtering in the July heat
—in my old Plymouth V8—
I
moved me and all my worldly shit
(four plastic bagsfull)
up Route 5 from L.A.
to
Berkeley

to become a writer

It was my third or fourth fresh start at sobriety
(not including jails and re-hab programs)
and
the goddamn Plymouth quit on me up a dusty side road
ten
miles
into
the
hottest
part
of
the
desert

114 degrees—

gushing water and exploded plastic everywhere

And all I owned—including my TV and two plants
stayed inside that baking car
for
over
a
week
until I could make it back and pay the tow truck guys

And today
beside my writing table—shading me from the afternoon Santa
Monica sun—
is the one plant that like me—
did
make
it

a goofy little schefflera
now seven feet tall and happy as a fat green cackling whore

Reminding me
That
on that
July outside Bakersfield
I wanted to quit
and
almost
did

but the Gods and a dumb plant had a better idea

POV

I know what it's like
to be outside
the circle
to be removed
unmagically

culled from the crowd

made an example of

turned
away

experiencing the sudden immediate emptiness
and the overpowering need to
dis-assemble

and never again re-appear

That's my trick, babee
my truth

time and again I've gone
poof
out of unreasonable
sometimes
completely unprovoked fear

Okay—hey wait—watch closely—I'll prove it

I'm a master
simply
stop loving me
and I promise
I'll
just
completely
disappear

genetics

Like booze
all the Fante's I know
gamble

an evil pitiless relentless obsession

My old man and
my dead brother Nick
and
my grandfather and his father too

boozers and gamblers all

and
now
me tooooooooooooooo

I now rot away my hours at internet poker—a slavering junky
—pissing away maxed-out credit card every cent

But wait! It's not all *that* bad
we Fante's are great storytellers too

It's
our only other
redeeming
feature

That
and
shit-brown
eyes

for A.L.

Find
someone else
who
will
hold the stars apart
for you—like I do

Some Basquiat-like
infant-minded chump
who'll say "yes"
out of fear
instead of
"no"

Fuck NO!

Because it is exactly because of loving you
that
I protect my heart
from your blackmail
and
the love songs I sing
in the bathroom
I sing to myself
in the shower or
taking a shit

You are my best friend
my evilest worst enemy
all
in a single breath

And I refuse to be tamed
by
your
uncompromising inexhaustible—confusing and unremitting
selfless
love

closing time

I know that you're gone
now
and all the rocks we threw and all the blood we spilled
today
will—in time—lose their sting
and become
unimportant

simply more dust down the road

Each of us will move on in our own way
me
with my stubborn and shameless sexual requests
and
you
to another man who is sober
and—christ knows
makes more money
and
better sense

And maybe in a few days
we'll talk on the phone again—about picking up clothes or forwarding
the mail—or even—by mistake—come face to face between the aisles
at the market in Venice we both like
or open a book some night and find a photo or some scraps of words
imprisoned
during the time
this thing we've killed
we said
would never end

But
most
of
all
I'll miss your quiet voice
and
the way you brushed your hair at night

those
precise
and
endless
two
hundred
strokes
just before we'd fuck like two crazed monkeys on the verge of
death and God

—and remember—

that we once began all this predictable
and
amazing
pleasure
and
pain
as
the best of friends

Iraq

The clouds this morning
driving over Topanga Canyon
to my new
phone-room-job
were
a white cotton tablecloth
against big Jesus' pepper blue work shirt

and
as I left the coast
driving into the hills
the fog lifted
and I gulped my coffee
and—for a change—
turned off my radio
(seems slick George has decided that enough is enough and these
towelheads will soon morph into a unilateral desert oil stain)
and

always proud to be an American

I tell myself

hey—it's all OKAY

I'm breathing in and out—right here
I'm free white and twenty-one—right
and
my precious national security is being guarded
by a soft-spoken gent who thinks nothing's wrong with
flaming out a few hundred thousand babies
for the small price of a 58% approval rating

Sure—no pain—no gain—right?

So thanks Dubya for your most singular vision of
unbuffered
unblemished
unimaginable
stupidity

And
by
the
way

when you have a second
from
your
busy
National Security
schedule

BLOW ME

sliding

Watching old Mom
fade out is atomic winter for me

powerlessness

blood
draining
a drop at a time
from an unseen wound deep here in my chest

Just months ago she was still reading five books a week
and torturing my sister day and night with her preposterous nagging
and crazy phone demands and accusations of every kind of
mad nonsense

And now at 91 she's suddenly slipped—like a blip on a screen—
like a lone cold spider disappearing into the snow

while outside her airless room
naturally—flawlessly—the red lights in L.A. still change to green
and life
like the endless bumper-to-bumper freeway traffic
continues to ooze on

And one day soon on some grassy patch under the ridiculous and
permanently blue California sky we'll bury her and stand around
uttering the kind of slop people utter over the dead
and the empty hole I feel now—this impending irredeemable chunk
of me
that I know now

will be gone forever

will be gone forever

and

Christ help me—I can already feel it—

I
know
now

that
I'll
give
just
about
anything
to
see
her
sweet
blue
eyes
again

fully recovered

Today
the girl sitting just in front of me
at the noon AA meeting
named Kelli
was wearing thronged panties

It's summer now in Venice
and every woman's garment
is designed to fit as tightly as possible
and
thronged
panties

are the sweet work of Satan

And the woman at the podium is slobbering on
about God and Step 9 and about how sorry she was
and about
clearing away the wreckage of her bankrupt dumbass past

with the kids in foster care and living under a freeway overpass for
eight months and parents who still refuse her phone calls

And
from time to time
Kelli in front of me
would bend to the floor to pick up her
foam coffee cup
and
thereby render the top and sides of those pink frilly—kill me dead
God—panties—again—to my full view

So
after the meeting
I said hi to a few people and got in line and smiled and thanked the
speaker for her talk
just as Kelli disappeared out the back door to the parking lot
never knowing
that I would've
signed over

49

my goddamn inheritance and all my credit cards
and my rent money
and the proceeds to my next five books
just

to be able to get
one look

at her
naked
in those
pink
frilly
pink
panties

in Paris

Out the window of the apartment
I see people on the boulevard
going up and down
busy
on their way to work
buying their paper
dodging traffic

And
just below me
a man and a woman at the café
chit-chat over a nine a.m. glass of wine
holding hands

while I'm thinking—Jesus here I am

propped up—a rusty old spoon in this big tub of sweet
mint
jam
on a free ride because of French TV and a book festival
feeling almost certain I belong—right here

And no cops will knock at my hotel door
and
the café waiter will smile and say bonjour when I order my espresso
and
all my bills are paid
and
the cigars I'll chew at the interview
today
will come in fat silver aluminum tubes

All I need to do is to keep breathing in and out
and not piss off my benefactors or be too frank with my compliments
to the braless mademoiselles
and
make myself believe that alla this—this magic flood of love
that fills me

51

to
nearly
bursting
a
once
crusted
over-medicated heart

is really me

and
no
pipe
dream

a celebrity

Tonight in Paris I met a famous French TV princess
who goes on and on about my art
in her e-mails
and
she is rich and once bedded down with Sartre
and meeting me has turned her seething essence into bliss

she says

she even quoted my smoldering translated shit to me—in French

And—hey—I always look forward to the free eats
and
when the time came

right after dessert

when she expected me to say something brilliant
about poetry
or twentieth century literature
or what drove me to years of madness and hopelessness
winding up with the taste of a rusty gun barrel in my mouth

I had no answers

And the TV princess looked hurt and disgusted
and—I'm sure—changed her mind about wanting me in the sack
but
that's okay
me and my mediocrity
will get by

We
still
have
our
price

a fool for love

Yesterday I made a bad error with an old girlfriend
Babette
after spilling her guts to me all afternoon
over too many scotch and cokes
about her lover boy who'd found out about this other guy
she'd been popping on the side a while back and (she says) she
never really cared about
but
holyshit—turns out the boyfriend broke a stack of dishes in her
kitchen hutch before snapping her door's hinge on his way out to the
Alibi Room in Culver City

So Babette wants to know what to do and what to say and how to
get mister right back
'cause now she knows it was really only him she loves
totally
exclusively
in
the
final
analysis

"You're the guy with the smart answers—so tell me what the hell is
supposed to happen now—I mean—what do I do?"

While considering a response I paid for the next round
then leaned across and whispered, "well, I think we should go back to
my place and catch up on old times"—then kissed her
wetly
on the neck

"Pig," she hissed

but two drinks later
she kissed me back
and said
"What the hell—okay, let's go"

And next morning
we're
both
awake—and sober
and
naked
and
Babette wants to borrow money to pay her electric bill
and take her cat to the vet

WAIT—THERE'S A MORAL HERE!

And that moral is:
cheap
advise
is
never
cheap

pulling teeth

Today we drove fifteen hours
from Paris to the beach in Rimini in Italy on our way to Potenza
for a literary festival
while—nonstop—I continue to plot the murder of the spoiled
French-twat-wife of this TV guy who is paying me to be in
his documentary

In the car the temperature is ninety-plus degrees
but she's insisting on having the windows up and no AC on
because—as it happens—the contessa-of-post-nasal-drip catches
chills easily from AC

Oh,
and she smokes too like everybody else in Europe
but cigarettes make her sick in a closed car
so, of course—there will be none of that

And the whole ride she's hissy at all of us and I'm trying to keep quiet
and restrain myself from lethally, terminally, insulting this ungodly
bitch—
with her capped teeth,
fake whiteblond hair
and three different pairs of pink-lensed sunglasses

Late in the afternoon—after six more sweaty pit stops
where I suck down quick Marlboros and continue to avoid eye contact
miss delightful
flounces back in the car in her newest snit regarding Italian gas
station bathrooms
then slams the seat back against my arm
that is currently holding a full cup of iced tea—
spilling the stuff all over me and my new $39 tan pants—
and says

NOW get this—"ohhhhhhhh . . . I guesss zat waz me"
not, hey I'm sorry—or kiss my ass—or geez—or fucking whoops, or
whatever but . . . ohhhhhh—just . . . ohhhhhhh

Later, after a shower and a damned decent dinner of pesto pasta—
alone in bed—

my brain does one of the personal historical surveys
it often feasts upon to prevent me from sleep
and
I realize
why—as a puking blackout drunk off and on for 15 years—
I used to fraternize
with the most ungodly bar sluts in the seediest joints in Manhattan

Because—see—as it turns out
the ugliest, skankiest, smelliest, New York slut
I ever met
was just way more amiable
than this French bitch
and I wouldn't mind if her and ten thousand more spoiled
gold-plated Parisian twats just like her—
got
buried
end-to-end
in concrete
under
the
Eiffel
fucking
Tower

for Anna

That night when we made it
for the first time in that loud hotel
in Milano
with our sudden greed to fuck and suck eachother
was—for me
like a wild birthday earthquake

Your cunt and asshole tasted so sweet and clean and opening wide
to my tongue
while the goddamn hallway doors kept slamming and the ice machine
outside groaned and people yakked by the elevator
and the junk on the nightstand began crashing everywhere
but nothing would stop us
and for twelve hours your breath and mine made one single sound

And when I whispered words like
turn around or does that hurt or lick me there or
can I cum in your mouth
you said—in Italian—your black Mediterranean eyes flaming—
"Do it—just do it—do whatever you like"

I
knew
that two thousand years of Rome and all the dead and mad martyred
saints had suddenly collected—
for me
in that room
in your smile

And I thought
bleeding Christ almighty—
let me die here and now
because this spell—this explosion of you and me—
this sudden arrival of unwarranted perfection
and all the reeling
vomiting volcanos of heaven and earth
are now pound pound pounding
out

love
and
death
at the same time—

for us

And nothing I will ever feel
will be—could be
one
bit
better
than
this

this you and me

in Hollywood

I'm in the office with Sid, this hotshit, 28-year-old
sky's-the-limit producer
and he's talking about making a movie from my book
and about how passionate and gut-level raw and real and in your face
my stuff is because—he predicts—"raw" WILL be *hot*
"sort-of like the way *Pulp Fiction* got hot all at once—
only for alkies, if ya know what I'm sayin"

And yeah, I say, I guess I know what you mean

Sid sees Bruno as a kind of a young hard-edged Travolta or shit—
maybe even Sean Penn—no kidding, Penn would be fuckin' perfect!!
And of course Sid knows his agent

And in comes no-bra Brandi
Sid's tall assistant with cappuccino the way
I like it and a note pad to jot stuff down—you know, just in case—

and Robert, Sid's director pal is there on the mauve leather couch
drinking fizzy water with lime
and Robert of course says he's read all my books

They *all* have—are you kidding?

And, yeah, though our life experiences are very different
because it appears
Robert is a Melrose Avenue pole smoker
he
can definitely relate to alienation and suicide and jail
and the demons that drive Bruno in the book
because Robert's got demons too . . . demons up-the-ass
—and our meeting goes on for another hour like that
and Sid thinks it'd be a good idea for me to go home and knock out
a strong first draft of the screenplay
and Robert agrees—don't you Robert—
and of course there's no up-front money for me—because—shit—
we're all just shooting in the dark here until we get something
that'll kick ass on paper—

"you get me the pages Fante and I'll do the rest"

And
all the way back to my dump in Venice
in my 16-year-old coughing Toyota I'm thinkin'
why don't I just go borrow the money and buy myself a gun and go
back there and kill these cocksuckers deader than filthy dead oinking
pigs for wasting half of my day and $3 worth of my precious
gas
money

for the comb-over lady

There's this old ghost
in
my
closet
and
for a hundred years I've kept it
quiet
like
whispering a secret
then waiting patiently for it to be betrayed by some frightened light

I've hauled my secret from house to house
and from wife to wife

all the winter days of my life

until

now

So here's my secret—in broad daylight

I've never really loved or cared about anyone
or anything
except myself
until
right now

until
you

expecting

So last night
after dinner
and yet another vital conversation
about health insurance
and joint accounts
and reducing interest rate credit card payments by balance
transference
and
making further plans for the upcoming expenses of the new arrival
basket-balling out
above the top of your
warm-up pants

I
walked outside to listen to the ocean
and
breathe in the June night air

and

stopped myself from saying the words:

I REALLY DON'T GIVE A SHIT—

that a moment before
had all but kamikazied out of my
fiscally insensitive mouth

And
realized
in a flash

under
the
stars

that this could easily be all gone
and
by birthright

a
guy
like me

should now be dead in a ditch like my crazy brother
instead of
saying what I should be saying
right now
which is

thank you
God

old news

Sometimes
a
deep
sink
hole
of aloneness
is
the price
for
being
a
writer

Before I know it—I'm over my head—strangled by it—
while
outside—outside my mind—a red and white hi-stepping marching
band goes by complete with Clydesdales and major-fuckin-ettes

and soundlessly I sit—a thorn ignoring the sun

Are all writers fools—arrogant isolationists
befuddled by themselves
believing that what they do entitles them to shiver alone
admiring their posing and overblown reflections

while admitting to nothing

Okay! Right!

I guess
that's
me

just don't tell any body

another goddamn Tuesday

I live in fear
these days
of the phone ringing
or clicking on
my e-mail

I owe everyone—some sort of payment
and a big bite out of my ass

They don't know
I've dried up
that my guts and balls and my heart reek of decay and dusty death
and
that
I can no longer tap tap tap
out anything of value
that
makes
any
sense or . . . means anything

So—next time—dial the coroner
for chrissakes
not
me
I'm all alone here
and wordless
just trying to survive the brutal conversation
crushing
my
mind

you and me and our two-bedroom palace

Today
in the sunshine of Playa Del Rey
looking toward the ocean

blinded by our new perfection

I stopped
standing still

a lizard on a warm spring wall

and
thanked
God
for
you

1:46 a.m.

Hey, you
fat saucer moon
be watchful
of those low-rent stars
in their cheap day-glo
slippers
skipping across your sky
attempting
to entice
some untrained astronomer's
eye

They're
jealous
fat moon
magnetized by the magic that is you

Let no one forget that your face in the chorus of vastness
is
substantiated evidence
that all we see and hear and touch and taste
and kiss
and resist

all

is part of
—not separate from—
your unwashed face
of
love

until last night

I belong to this group
of so called—Twelve Step Hollywood Writers—
which is to say
not real writers at all
but ex-drunk
hack
screenwriters

the simpering complaining—often human looking—
zombie stand-ins for actual breathing—blood and guts writers

For three Mondays in a row I've spent my evenings sitting in a metal
chair slurping coffee and listening to these over-paid self-satisfied
Benz-driving wannabes bleating out whiney syllables of snot about
producer rejection and not getting this or that sit-com "picked up" or
the "agonizing" waiting and waiting—between assignments

Finally someone called on me—asked me to contribute
something
wanted to know how it was going for me
and
what I heard my mouth say was, I don't know about you but I love
what I do—I'd be dead if I couldn't write
as
dead as you lifeless ungrateful flim-flam wannabe make-believe
screenwriter assholes

Then—all the way driving home I kept kicking my own ass
and un-congratulating myself on the ease with which I kill off
friendships

Yeah, I'm tired of being the only snarling black dog in the room
but Christ knows it's too late for me to learn how to play nice
like the rest of the blow job starlet boys
at L.A.'s writer's meetings

wayyy too late

for you

Okay
it's true
I can't get you out of my head

27 and a black-eyed Puerta Rican
and somehow never been in the sack with a man
or—a woman

And
I remember in that hotel room
while you were taking off your shirt
I was pulling your jeans down too

You never even blinked
and
there you were
—ready

I'd honestly forgotten how sweet that sweet stuff can be

And even when there was blood everywhere
that was okay too
because we just kept at it
until
I knew that you were the best thing that has happened to me
since I got that half-assed good review in the L.A. *Times*

And next morning after coffee near the IRT station
as we kissed I was the one who didn't want any of it to end
or say goodbye

Well, it hasn't—it can't
you're alive and well and in my mind and in my jockeys
and
when all's said and done
at my age
I guess I'd just about give up
anything

for
one
more
taste
of
that
sweet
sweet
peach
pie

FFF

Butterfly
fly over batter
fly faster
than the chatter
of those that are sure they truly matter

Butterfly
you don't fly
you flutter
you flow on a breeze
far safer
than my thoughts
that are fastened to the faucet of
of more fear
than
laughter

Butterfly
wind dancer
face your maker
every flap you flap
lasts forever

lasts forever

Arizona Highway

Sick to death of L.A.
sick of the 24-7 bumper to bumper traffic
and the combustible constant driveby rage
of even my neighbors

and desperate for a change . . . to anything

me and THE BOSS
made the half-day weekend ride to Sedona

That sundown on the main drag—highway 89A—downtown
the air was stingingly clean
and
we could see for a hundred miles in any direction
where a dozen towering rock castles stood off in the distance
like the cartooned boots of God's army

And she looked over at me
and smiled

I
could
live
here—THE BOSS said

Hearing the words gave me a shiver—because—see—I've finally come
to understand that women know instinctively—about almost
everything—there is to know about children and homes and domestic
tranquility
and all that ever-so-vital shit

So—next morning I surrendered—signed the check—and left a deposit
on that big joint on Piki Drive—and we began a new life

And that—as they say—was that

no more

I just read Thursday Morning's E-Mail
and
vowed to myself that
I'm done writing blurbs for other writers on the backs of mediocre
books
I
really could care less about—

done
doing favors then feeling bloated with disgust for my exaggerations—
and feeling like a fraud

done being a nice guy—I'm not a nice guy

done trying to say appropriate and supportive
shit
about shit
that I don't think is either appropriate or supportable

done done done

Done supplying free stories and poems to on-line magazine editors
who have the balls to ask for my stuff
then confide they cannot yet afford to pay for it

Done with that too! Screw that!

But there's one thing I'm not yet done doing
and that thing that I am not done doing
is
writing angry poems

I'm not yet
done
doing
that
not yet

Giovanni at two

Give that back
No—put that down and get away from there

Listen!

Jesus, TWO! What an amazing age
for discovery—dismemberment—and destruction

Helplessly I watch out of one eye as trouble enters my office
while I write

I watch where it goes—what it touches—what objects must fall
which are moved
what containers dumped
which wastebaskets and pencil and paperclip cups topple
which light plugs are pulled then replugged
then tasted

I am a father again
revisiting parenthood
without cigarettes and bourbon

at peace most days

present for the parade
and for a life
full of brand new colors

Jesus
what an honor

One last chance
not
to
screw
things
up

a true thespian

I'm UP again
today at seven o'clock at Midnight Special Book Store
in Santa Monica

doing
my
writer
act

again

putting on my tie and my best unscuffed shoes
to dance
my dumb dumbo bear dance
and
try again
to get used to the feeling of having my penis measured in public
exposing my guts and soul as a writer—
smiling when I want to run instead

So—hey—if you're around—come sit in and listen up –
maybe
even
buy
a
book

and know that I'll
just
be
standing
there
bleeding
to
death inside

one
red drop at a time

July 4th, 2006

Somedays
I'm scared to death
that
you'll wake up and realize you're married to
a halfdead—soon-to-be—social security recipient
and
that some dusty afternoon I'll walk through the garage and your car
won't be there
and
you
and our kid and my bank account and my heart and my guts
will all be gone
packed and off—
down some hot summer Arizona road
with
Bob—the white-toothed T-shirt stud from Safeway
who never fails to leer at you as he bags the bread and milk

Back to L.A.
or New York
and that acting career you gave up to be with me

I mean—why not
I'm bad tempered
vain
stubborn
thin-skinned
and
insecure

tired, talentless, and burned-out

an also ran

second-rate at almost everything I've ever done
except
for
loving you

June 15, 2006

Opening the note from my brother Jim
I learned today that I'm the one he blames—hates even—for this new
L.A. Times article
about me and the old man
that asserts
John Fante was a drunk
a depressive asshole—a nut
and
a
rager

Seems—just for a change—
"You've thrown pop's reputation under the bus"

Jim's years younger than me and was not around
as his father's pre-diabetic pre-sobriety fireworks were going off
blasting skyward

never saw—or felt—Daddy's collateral damage
never saw him piss on the livingroom carpet
or crash through the coffee table
and rap his car around a tree

To brother Jim—John Fante was a smiling sit-com dad
a little league baseball coach
a par golfer—a prince
a genuine stand-up guy

Right—swell—absolutely

And
I'm
the
fucking
King
of
Siam

culture jock

I'm not at all well known in America
I mean
nicely anonymous describes me nicely
but
in Italy I've published a few books
and
a play too

But
mostly people know me through my father's work
I'm Fante junior—the other Fante—the angry recovered alcoholic
derelict

But even with that I'm still half-assed famous
and always shocked when I step off the plane
in Milano or Rome and some guy with a TV camera asks a thousand
un-translated rehashed questions

and the next morning I see a snapshot of my mug in the daily paper

and I light my cigar and rock back in a chair that often overlooks a
Venice canal
and watch as the waitress or desk clerk checks me out

I mean this ain't America
In Italy I'm a somebody—
I'm half assed famous—I matter

and my very next thought is: no kidding
now
will
someone
please
pass
the
salt

the desert

Out on the Mojave
deep into Route 40
three hundred miles from L.A.
and
any
man-made
thing
beneath a blanketed blue sky

the road is straight
unfaltering
and all things alive—live undisturbed

all

feels
possible—entirely simple

Here the only evil that kills that which cannot defend itself
is
thought

Here—harmless fear
waits by the side of the road
like a rotting tire
guarding the minimum speed limit

Here
I see clearly and simply the difference
between
the truth
and the jiveass nonsense I make up

—the death and the life between my ears—

Here—for an instant—it's okay to be a transient
truly—actually—honestly

on my way
for
a
visit
with
God

July 9th, 2006

Long after midnight
an airless—brilliant
full Sedona moon
filled
the bedroom window

So bright
the clouds glowed
and
their silver edges
shook
in the sky
like the gleam of a thousand
tossed
plates
trapped in flight

Searching for a sleeping hand
on the sheet next to mine—I held it to me—
and
watched the miracle of life and death

breathe in and breathe out

celebrating
the silent chilling joy
of
loving
you

don't ask me

My pal Bill
a fine
fine poet
and a bonifide freakazolid ex-drunk New York nutjob

sent me an e-mail note today

Seems he's all dried up
his stuff
"feels"
derivative
and—he wants to know—

what the hell do I do when it's like that for me

My fingers didn't miss a beat:
I keep going—I say back—
I write right through the walls and the bricks and the mind crap
that blocks me
good—bad—and miserable
I just keep going
because

and here's the real truth

I'm afraid to quit

If I do I might get drunk again
or kill my dog
or have to face the sleeping monster
behind my eyes

I write because it is what is between me and death
and I sure as shit don't want to check out
one second before
I'm recognized as the greatest breathing genius of
my generation
and that—I tell him—is just exactly how crazy I am

why me

Another unsolicited manuscript today
in my mail box
this one from a twenty-two year old female in Beverly Hills
tumbling out at me like a four-hundred-and-eighty-seven-page
terrorist threat—an uncoiling snake

a goddamn novel about dating . . .

You gotta be kidding—about dating!

Why me . . . I mean I never "dated" anyone
the bitches I've known
my hostages were all cornered
in parking lots after last call
we were vampires
consuming eachother's body parts
then staggering off to a wine-soaked dawn

But now I'm beginning to understand what comeuppance means
the notion of karma
these waves of retribution that come my way
for my years of frivolous dalliances because
it now appears
that for **each** woman I kicked out—or **each** male I screwed in some
evil phone scam—
I will now receiving one ungodly—brutal and hideously written
manuscript—until my debt to the Gods is paid in full

I promised myself years ago—like my old man—to never turn
another writer away—
but Jesus
some of what I get in the mail these days is so bad
I don't know whether
to
shit
or
go blind

the last—last call

Tommy Miller
checked
out
the other day—Wednesday—I got the call from his sister Lynda

And later that day I gashed my goddamn hand patching a hole in the
garage wall

He was fifty-three
a writer wannabe and a golf-course hustler and a bad bad gambler
and a mean, incurable pill head, like his Moms
who got her ticket punched the same way thirty years ago

Blood was running down my arm and the slash scared the old lady
enough that she had to wrap it in a towel and get me to the ER for
twelve stitches

And me and Tommy grew up babysitting each other while our dads
roamed 1950's L.A.
gambling at the Garden Of Allah and being Hollywood goof-offs
together

Lynda says they found him in a twenty-dollar Culver City motel—
unresponsive—

I mean people die every day—right—
and the gash in my arm
and in my heart will heal . . . eventually
right

but goddamnit Tommy—goddamn you—leaving me and us like this
what a goddamn waste
not even a fresh poem on the table or a note by the phone—
nothing—
not shit
just empty script pill bottles and puke and the curtains of a dark room
drawn tight
and dirty unmade sheets

4/2/93

Pieces of me
long gone
are back

Places inside that were
far too far
away
to ever want to touch

lost tunes

have words again
and
are
brand new

I'm a boy on my bike again
lost to spring
speeding through the side-streets of open New York fire hydrants
soaking wet
tossing my life to a God
who skips rope in heaven

I've learned to
somehow
at this ripe old age
believe
completely
in
the
here
and
now

another fat Tuesday

Anna Banana called today—drunk—to tell me that three weeks ago
she spent seventy-two hours in a hospital ward in Culver City

She fell again—she says
drunk as a dog—again
this time knocking herself cold on her backdoor concrete steps
with her top front teeth breaking off and puncturing her lip
then—hours later—waking up in a lake of thick sticky blood
and calling 9-1-1—and the EMT guys
who eventually show up and mop up

But hey it's all okay now
she's home and feeling fine—and the up side is she went almost two
weeks without a drink—until today
and her face surgery went okay and her brother the dentist'll fix those
two top teeth up just fine and hey—Danny-boy—maybe you could
stop by again some time soon
ya know
like the old days—and remember that purple camisole and panties
you bought me that time and that tattoo place we stopped at on
Venice Beach and that guy Stevie with the fat old Rottie pooch

Ann's pretty drunk and finally confesses that hey, this stuff's getting
pretty scary—I mean shit, I almost bled to death—and—tell me the
truth Danny-boy, do you ever think about us and the fun we
used to have

I do Ann—I say—I sure do—but look, I gotta go here—I'm on a
deadline with this thing I'm writing and my cat's in the other room
knocking books and stuff off the shelves and making a goddamn
mess—but good to talk to you

yeah, you too Danny-Boy—take care my sweetie pie
. . . I love you . . . I sure do

Me too Annie—me too—I love you too

here ya go Pop—this one's for you

Today I got an e-mail
a John Fante fan letter e-mail—
that clicked up an old memory
about how years ago—one summer—
I came back to L.A. from New York and my nighttime cab driver gig
to my old man's home in Malibu
carrying my suitcase full of books
drunk as a monkey from hours of dollar-a-shot airplane booze

I was a genius in those days—a lyrical fraud—
reading my turgid shit at night in coffee houses on Second Avenue
where Dylan and a thousand other Kerouac stylized wannabes—
like me—performed with deathly earnestness prior to the upcoming
war-ending revolution that somehow never happened

And John Fante was a nobody—an aging diabetic has-been busted
out—out-of-print—second string Hollywood screenwriter
killing time in the social security line

One morning toward the end of my two weeks of mooching his booze
the old man threw a paper-clipped manuscript on the breakfast table
and lit his pipe—"Read that hot shot," he says

—the book was: *1933 Was A Bad Year*—

Slurping at my coffee I looked up and
said sure—but what is it

—Pop's black Italian eyes blazed—I finished it last week he said—and
it's ten times better than any of those brilliant assholes you're always
bragging about

juss read it for chrissakes—

So I did—I spent the day in the shade of his back patio—sipping rose
wine and smoking Lucky cigarettes and flipping those sacred pages

and coming away

stunned
having nearly forgotten
that my father was precisely who he said he was

a master at words—a prince on paper

And it didn't matter to Pop who knew it or didn't know it
because he knew it —always knew it—he'd tattooed it—
deep deep in his heart and in his bones

So today
after reading my John Fante e-mail fan letter
my heart got re-filled and re-flooded with the proud memory
of the symphonies of brilliance left behind on the bookshelves above
my head—my inheritance
and the knowing that all I have to do is open one of his books
or turn a page
to once again feel
like
the
richest
man
alive

daylight

I was rowing a boat
in my dream last night
sailing around and around the same
borderless
bottomless
black lake
filled with the evil evil faces of the fatuous fish
—the thousand people I have known
and
hated

my hit list

And some of these scaly monsters even attempted to dive into my
spotless craft
anxious to shout out the litany of my failures and faults
while I—still rowing—pretended not to listen

Finally
after beating these fat-eyed pricks off I congratulated myself
for defeating their
pious
pigsnot

But then—waking up—looking around
I reassessed and reconsidering this dream
only to find myself
deeply dissatisfied
because
one of those faces

—your face—
was still there next to me
on
my
pillow

Sonoma

We walked
between endless rows of wet trees
the afternoon wine country sun
deafening above us

a sopping sheet

moving us
—branch by branch—
away from
eachother

Finally
uselessly
I wanted—began to try—to say I'm sorry
but instead
decided on picking a perfect handful of grapes
then offering them to you
and the Gods of what
you last night—still called love

Go ahead—I thought
it's true
I drink too much—and I can't stop it or help it—
hate me and mail in your puritan pity
I'd rather pound cheap Chablis all afternoon
and
die
alone
than
cheat an orchard
of
my
honesty

what?

I'll be honest here
okay

I mean—most of the time
I
have no idea what's up—what I'm doing

I seem to operate clue-less-ly

instinctively

uncertainty appears to be what I do best
at least
looking backward
creatively
job wise and wife wise and career-wise and child wise

unless
I give myself a specific task
a check list
like mailing a letter or buying trash bags at Vons
or a quart of oil
I've
just always seemed to bump into things

all my life

then
wonder why at my ripe old age

I've become as happy
and
as
dumb
as
I
am

hitting the big time

Okay, I guess now I must really be famous
because
this week, I'm back in Paris giving a TV interview and talking to this
guy from *Liberation Magazine*
and this "girl" whose been sending me hot e-mails for a year
wanting to know about writing and poetry and my old man
and this and that—calls me at my friend's flat
and says
can we have a drink together

I've never seen her before
but when I get to the bistro
there's no mistake
she's twenty-nine and decked out in tight jeans and high-heeled
pink pumps
and her braless nipples push push push against the pockets of an
open black-silk blouse

And later that night
after we've spent all that sweaty afternoon
together
going at it like two unappeasable dogs feasting upon eachother's
parts
and
I'm back in my room alone
I check my pants pocket—counting my money—
and estimate roughly that when I get back to L.A. at the end of the
month
I'll have a grand total of 75 or 80 dollars left—
plus change—
along with the two hundred bucks that currently clogs my lean
checking account

And
of course
the rent will be due
and
all the other stuff

and
my newest career plan is maybe to go back selling cars again
or hit an office supplies boiler room
in Hollywood—
and to
just keep on keeping on a roof above my head

Ah fame!
ain't it a bitch

summer sky

Sedona
is
a
star-gazers
black
planetarium at night

I find (and soften) my heart
every time
I stare deep
within the sky's blanket of beauty

and then
begin to gulp in the notion of
just
how
ridiculous and overwhelmingly stupid
it is
for
me
to
make
any
plans
at
all

Buddy

Michelangelo Giovanni Fante is now 2 1/2
and this morning his mom looked at me over the rim of her coffee cup
and said
"what that kid needs is a dog—boys need a friend—a pal"

So—obedient chump that I am
we saddled up and all three of us
—after phone calls and missed streets and wrong turns—
found the Sedona Animal Shelter
wherein
reside over a hundred of the loudest
yappingest barkingest lickingest neediest
strays
ever imprisoned behind wire and concrete

And there was Buddy
a two-year-old ninety-pound black and white pit bull/lab mix
who licked Ayrin's cheek and kissed my face
then
knocked Giovanni
on his ass
making him cry and sending him scared stiff back into his Mom's
arms

So that was that—done deal
I hated leaving Buddy behind because me and that dog
connected

And on the way home it came to me that I'd learned a new and
valuable lesson: never ever disagree or cross swords with a mom
who believes she's protecting her baby
unless of course you enjoy
spending a night or two sleeping on a bumpy leather couch

playing it safe

Sometimes
for me
on the border between
reality and insanity
stands
my
pen

and the *knowing* that honest passion necessitates an end to lies
and . . . compromise

When my gut tells me to say it
then I must spit it out
and sometimes puke those flames directly into God's face

and
then be willing to face what comes next
whatever that is

A poet's silence is an act of terrorism
and it is his pen
that slashes the poison from the world's wounds
and insures
aid
and
comfort
to saying
what is often

the unsayable

at 3 a.m.

In the dream
I'm squinting
watching a brutal sun melting
dripping
down
the
tallest
hardest
blood-spattered busted-up cinderblock wall

into a gooey crushed unkindness

and
all courage is gone
and love is dead and vengeance is master
and I'm completely alone—in pain—
and the winners
—all the other combatants—naturally—
sashay in triumph on George Bush-purchased kevlar horses
celebrating my imminent humiliation
as they watch
me
being dipped headlong—again and again—
into the tallest most putrescent pit of the thousand worst poems I've
ever written

Until finally—waking up—
I realize—YO look—my stuff really can't be all that bad—
I mean half a life filled with 12-Step Meetings and 29 dollar motels
and suicide attempts and a handful of ex-wives and mounting
insurmountable IRS debt has to tally up to something—
some kinda middle-of-the-night meaning

I'm hoping that beauty *really* is in the eye of the beholder unless of
course it's true that God is just out there somewhere pointing down—

keeping track—
laughing
his
fat
ass

peace & freedom

My pal Charlie
is some kinda famous hi-techie right-wing
magazine cover computer geek
and undercover national security genius

no-kidding—a very scary guy
who
definitely
knows
his
stuff

And every once in while Charlie tells me just what's up
in America . . . surveillance-wise
about how the new bar codes in your Walmart sports shirt
can satellite track your ass as it moves around the world to within a
meter of where you step next

don't matter if it's in Compton or friggin' Tai Pei

And how your cell phone
is nothing more than a built-in FBI/CIA cop doggie collar
allowing all your communications to be monitored twenty-four seven
by some administration Taliban-hating cracker with a mean hangover
and a pair of fifty-dollar headphones

And all this you say is
just
paranoia

Right—Absolutely

Go tell
that
to
Charlie

reunion

saw my old drinking bud Lillie today—in—of all places
–Vons Market
with her new blue dress on
and her nails done
red
red
red
and fresh from a job interview that she didn't get

I'm in line at the checker and half-ass didn't recognize her
until she smiled her smile

She'd been a looker once
and a hooker off a corner of Santa Monica Boulevard
in
my limo days

She's forty four now—goin' on seventy-four
and trying the straight life again
after doing a nickel at Chowchilla
and losing both her kids and livin' downtown at The Cecil

It was always Lillie's smile that got me
that—I love ya forever sixty-cent smile
and
the reminder
an hour later
back home sitting at my keyboard

that it's the heart behind the eyes that
never
ever
goes
away

for Arthur

In the middle Sixties
I did a lot of my drunken hack driving in the South Bronx
and Harlem
scary shit—in a very scary place

hard and deadly dark streets

And in those days almost none of the white drivers at my garage
—on 146th Street—
would pick up blacks
except me and Arthur—crazy Arthur
the maddest knife-carrying most brilliantly articulate nigger and white
hating sonofabitch I'd ever met
except
when he'd get drunk with me and we'd laugh
together and guzzle 10-High whiskey out of cardboard cups at three
a.m. behind the liquor store on Girard Avenue
howling our asses off until
the sun came up—about books—and politics—and poetry—
and Viet Nam and Lyndon fuckin' Johnson and Huey Newton

And here it is forty years later
and I hadn't thought about Arthur
for years until just now—today
when my little son Gio smiled up at me
that same kind of goofy beaming cockeyed smirk he used to smirk

So god damn you Arthur
you just made me cry for you
and wish—
just once—
this one time—
we could laugh that way again

NO NO NO NO NO NO

Ten years ago—between writing novels—I wrote a new play
about my old man, John Fante
and called it DON GIOVANNI
and sent it out
and sent it out
and sent it out

And it was like I'd written the piece in Chinese or Farsi
or Sandskrit or some goddamn thing 'cause nobody cared

not one blink of interest—not anywhere

Then, in my spare time, I rewrote DON GIOVANNI once or twice
more and added more conflict and more humor and more madness
and . . . sent it out again . . . everywhere

And guess WHAT

nobody cared—not one blink of interest anywhere—zippo!

So that was that
I dumped all the copies of the play into my filing cabinet's
bottom drawer and chalked the whole deal off as a waste of time
until—nine years later
when I was in Italy and a newspaper guy—a friend—who didn't know
I wrote plays—asked to read it—then wrote back
how staggeringly brilliant a writer I am and how he wants to do a
national tour of DON GIOVANNI and then take it to New York and
The West End in London . . .

So okay—now here's the moral: Always remember you're a goddamn
genius no matter what anybody says and do not listen to experts or
producers or critics or your old lady
and keep smoking those sixty Camels a day and swindling the IRS
and watching your internet porn
but
keep writing
for chrissakes—just keep writing—just never give up or stop writing

3-22-07

What
you
think
you
know

is just that

thought . . . and bullshit

What
Really
is

is
what you *experience*

what
actually
touches
your
heart

28 years sober

O'Brien was from The Bronx
and had
the ability
to invariably
piss people off
and make 'em hate him and make 'em squirm

He was old and off booze longer then God
and had become a page and paragraph scholar of alkie literature and
had memorized all the books
which only deepened his arrogance and sarcasm and intolerance
of all humanity

I'd often bump into O'Brien
at evening meeting around L.A.
his finger'd be in some just-sober alkie's face—evangelizing about
sobriety and the AA Big Book—
or giving hell to the meeting leader for not doing this
or that procedure right

About three weeks before he kicked off from lung cancer
he was looking like a sunken ghost
and me and some of the other guys
took the old sonofabitch to dinner at Norm's in Santa Monica
and I asked him
"So, howya doin' Ken"

O'Brien coughed for about a minute
"Not bad for a dead man" he sneered—"I think I'll get myself one of
those weight loss lapel buttons that reads, *I lost sixty pounds—ask
me how*"

But he never complained once
and there were 800 sober ex-drunks at his funeral
most of 'em half-afraid he might just jump out of his coffin
and tell the priest
how to run the service
because

sure as hell

there
was
one
guy
who

didn't go the big meeting in the sky

in peace

change

Pain
has been my greatest—most powerful—and really—only teacher

through the divorces
and
job losses and car wrecks
and
jails
and SWAT Team relationships with crazy bitches
nothing
has ever crushed me
as
much
as my
own bad choices
and brutal
screaming
careless
stupidity

These days it's not so much that I'm changed from being a boozer
I'm not

I
just learned
to say uncle
and now—unmedicated—
the price difference
between
a
white
flag
and
a
toe
tag

facing Tuesday

I woke up sick today
coughing
and
snorting

bones raw and bruised
from christ-knows-what
hideous
inhaled
microscopic
invasive
little-shit-bug monster

feeling like the old days—the morning after I'd fallen down in a bar
or failed at another flight of stairs

ass over boot heel

then gone to bed
—happy and slobbering—
feeling nothing
until
the
next
morning

So half an hour later
downstairs
I
snarled at the old lady because the coffee was cold
and swatted the kid's butt for—one more time—coloring on the same
leather couch after I'd told him a thousand times
to knock it off

And making matters worse
my accountant called
to let me know that I'd neglected to declare a nine-thousand dollar
check
from publishing royalties last year
and

don't you know that that's exactly
the kind of red flag omission
that'll get you in trouble again with the IRS

Then—sitting down to write
nothing
comes out
except a chilled twenty-year-old memory
of holding
the barrel of my Charter Arms .38 against the roof of my mouth
then clicking the hammer back
and
thinking
why not?

Why the hell NOT

And the answer came back—
BECAUSE
because there just might be something more

And it turns out I was right
there is something more
it's
called

a new goddamn
IRS
audit

10-11-06

When
I
forget
who
I
am
I
trust
no
one

When
I
know
who
I
am

I
am
with
God

Thursday

That's right
it's gone—you spent it last night—pissed it away—again
and
down the hallway—through the door—you can hear
the coughing
and the whispered voices
of what's being said—the lies and excuses—
to
the manager guy
as
he—door by door
knocks
knocks
knocks
and walks
his
way along the hardwood floor
toward
your
room

That's right, champ—this is it
—Thursday—Pay Up Day—again
and the lies you now must tell better'd be the ones
—your best lies—
that'll keep you alive

allow you to survive
until
8:00 a.m.

with your sanity and your last ten bucks

when—thank Christ

the
bars
reopen

saying goodbye

They're both in the ground
now
under the same
hard
too simple
carved
flat stone

—the old man years ago
and just today—
Mom
at
ninety-one

Standing there
waiting for my mouth to mouth something

some kind of benediction

wisdom from the eldest surviving son—the writer in the family—

then ending up speechless
like
a
crushed
smile

(I expect too much from words
when what is
really
required
is
silence
the unsayable)

Soooooooooooooooo
so long Mom
I wish I could remember your song

because all I'm
left

with
now
is the memory of
those last crushing months
when death creeped closer and closer
and
the minutes got so long
that
I somehow forgot
to say
I
love
you

one for the gipper

After
the
reading
in
London

there she is

a
goddamn
10

British-Chinese mix
or Asian and something else

about twenty-five

in—of all things—a form-fitting Tim Hasselbach New York Giants
football jersey
and skintight black pants

with
a glass
of
wine
and her green-eyed Cockney charm
propelling
her
my way

"So are you really like that—"
she whispered
"all those sexual
dirty things you write about"
her tits pushing against the arm of my jacket

I waited a full half minute before answering
because—I've discovered that drunk women at readings
usually want a writer to have something
searing or wise up his sleeve

So finally I said
"I'm staying at The Groucho—are you ready to find out"

"Oh my God," she smiled, "you're quite the nasty old bastard"

"I guess maybe I am," I said
"But my question to you is; are we talking or screwing at The Groucho
this evening"

She rolled her eyes, stepped back, then finished her glass in one
swallow

"Will you sign a book for me"

"Sure—at the hotel," I said

"I'm afraid that's not possible"

So I took her book, autographed it, then handed it back

And she looked pleased and grateful until she read the signature

"Hey, you're not John Grisham," she said

"And you ain't Tim-fuckin'-Hasselbach"
I said back

the Santa Monica Freeway—tooooo p.m.

The guy
in the chrome-bumpered pick-up truck with the Harley Davidson
sticker in the window
just
ahead of me
on my right

didn't signal

and—while yakking on his cell phone—changed lanes
damn near
taking my fender off

So I honked—and honked
—jesus Christ man—hang up and pay attention for chrissakes—whaz
your problem

and

hit the gas pedal
passing
him in the dust

Until
a second later he's back
whizzing passed me
gesturing—flashing mad yellow teeth and delivering the one-finger
salute

What else can I do—I hit the gas pedal—swing wide—
then pull up to his passenger window

Hey—I yell—are you crazy or what!

And from under his seat Captain Koo-koo pulls a section
of metal pipe
and at seventy miles an hour
begins waving it

yelling

PULL OVER MOTHERFUCKER—I'LL RIP YOUR HEAD OFF AND

SHOVE IT UP YOUR ASS

And just thirty seconds ago I'm driving along—
humming away with Van Morrison

watch the bubbles come up in the water

and now zingo!
like a TV cop show—my life is on the line

So
welcome pilgrim
say hello
to
Wednesday
afternoon
in Los Angeles, California

where
blood and lives are cheap
and the bad dreams you never dreamed could come true

suddenly
come
true

BOOKS BY SUN DOG PRESS

Steve Richmond, *Santa Monica Poems*

Steve Richmond, *Hitler Painted Roses*
(Foreword by Charles Bukowski and afterword by Mike Daily)

Steve Richmond, *Spinning Off Bukowski*

Neeli Cherkovski, *Elegy for Bob Kaufman*

Randall Garrison, *Lust in America*

Billy Childish, *Notebooks of a Naked Youth*

Dan Fante, *Chump Change*

Robert Steven Rhine, *My Brain Escapes Me*

Fernanda Pivano, *Charles Bukowski: Laughing With the Gods*

Howard Bone with Daniel Waldron, *Side Show: My Life with Geeks, Freaks & Vagabonds in the Carny Trade*

Jean-François Duval, *Bukowski and the Beats*

Dan Fante, *A gin-pissing-raw-meat-dual-carburetor-V8-son-of-a-bitch from Los Angeles*

David Calonne, Editor, Charles Bukowski, *Sunlight Here I Am: Interviews and Encounters, 1963-1993*

Ben Pleasants, *Visceral Bukowski, Inside the Sniper Landscape of L.A. Writers*

Chandler Brossard, *Over the Rainbow? Hardly*
(Introduced and edited by Steven Moore)

Dan Fante, *Short Dog*

BOOKS BY DAN FANTE

Chump Change

Mooch

Spitting Off Tall Buildings

A gin-pissing-raw-meat-dual-carburetor-
V8-son-of-a-bitch from Los Angeles

Short Dog (aka Corksucker)

Don Giovanni

Dan Fante began his writing career in his mid-forties after many years as a drunk. "I went to a Christmas party in 1964 and sobered up sometime in the first week of January, 1986," says Fante.

Fante writes poetry, plays, short stories and novels. He is currently at work on a cable television adaptation of his book of short stories, *Short Dog*. He lives in Sedona, Arizona with his wife Ayrin and his son, Michelangelo Giovanni Fante. Fante vows never to return to the city of Los Angeles except at gunpoint or for the purpose of cremation.

Dan Fante's books have been translated into many foreign languages.